D is for Dinosaur

COLORING BOOK

Ken & Mally Ham

D is for Dinosaur Coloring Book

Ken & Mally Ham

First printing: October 2016
Third printing: April 2021

Copyright © 2016 by Ken & Mally Ham. All rights reserved. No part of this book may be used or reproduced in any manner whatsoever without written permission of the publisher, except in the case of brief quotations in articles and reviews. For information write:
Master Books®, P.O. Box 726, Green Forest, AR 72638
Master Books® is a division of the New Leaf Publishing Group, Inc.

ISBN: 978-1-68344-015-4

Unless otherwise noted, Scripture quotations are from the New King James Version of the Bible. Please consider requesting that a copy of this volume be purchased by your local library system.

Printed in the United States of America

Please visit our website for other great titles:
www.masterbooks.com

For information regarding author interviews,
please contact the publicity department at (870) 438-5288.

Master Books®
A Division of New Leaf Publishing Group
www.masterbooks.com

A is for Answers

A is for **Answers** from God's Holy Book;
Just open the pages and take a good look.
God created the earth, in space it did hang;
Creation's first day, without a BIG BANG.

B is for Bible

B is for **Bible**, where it says on day 2,
God made the clean air for me and for you.
He divided the waters above and below;
Day 3 comes next, so there we shall go.

C is for Continent

C is for **Continent**, the first dry land,
Which God had made by His Powerful hand.
Then He commanded that all the plants grow;
The third day was truly a beautiful show.

D is for Dinosaur

D is for **Dinosaur**, but you'll have to wait,
'Cause on day four other things God did make.
He formed the sun, the stars, and the moon.
Are you ready? We'll see those dinosaurs soon!

E is for Everything

E is for Everything that swims in the seas,
Made on day five, with the birds in the trees.
He also created the great Plesiosaur;
Reading God's Word, we can know this for sure.

F is for Fantastic

F is for Fantastic – that's all we can say,
As we see what God made on this, the sixth day!
Adam and Eve and the pouched kangaroo;
The rest of the animals and dinosaurs, too.

G is for Garden

G is for the **Garden** God specially made,

Where Adam and Eve could always have stayed.

Living in Eden, a world without sin;

What a beautiful place for them to live in.

H is for Hungry

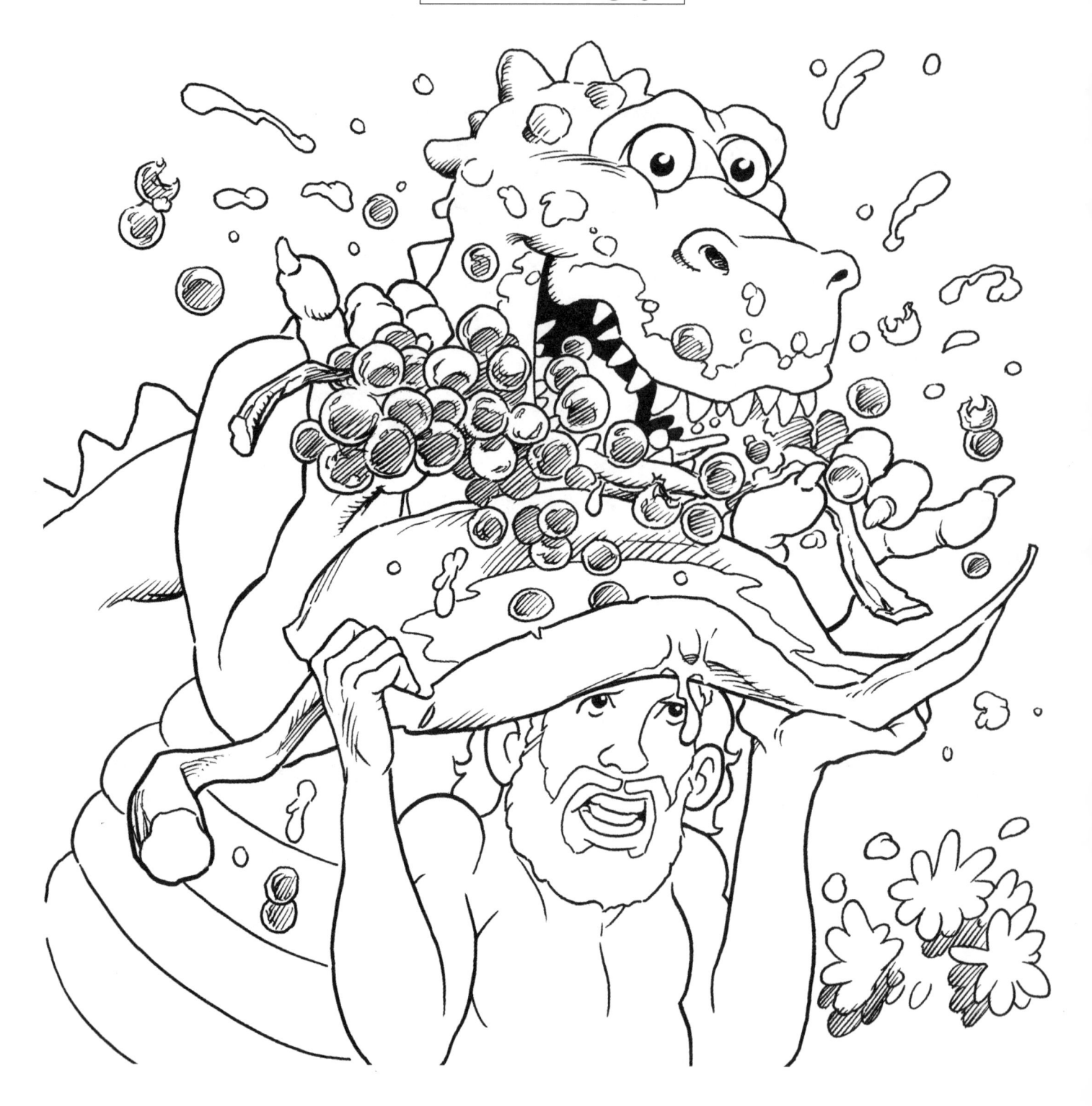

H is for Hungry, it's how we describe

A big dinosaur with his mouth open wide.

Adam wasn't scared to watch dinosaurs eat,

Because all the creatures ate plants, hand not meat.

I is in s"i"n

I is the letter in the middle of s"i"n,
To remind us all of the trouble we're in.
Dinosaurs, people, and the whole universe;
Because of man's sin, God judged with a curse.

J is for Just

J means **Just** awful – I'm sure we could say
The effects of sin grew worse every day.
Flesh became violent, the Bible reveals.
Were people and creatures now dinosaur meals?

K is for Knowledge

K is for **Knowledge**, which made Noah sad;

The world would be judged, because people were bad!

God warned he would send a terrible flood

That would cover the world with water and mud.

L is for Listen

L is for Listen: Noah knew that he should,

As soon as God said, "Make an ark out of wood.

Take each land animal, two-by-two;

Your family's among the hard-working crew."

M is for Monster

M is for Monster like the great dinosaur;
But how could he enter the ark through the door?
Well, many dinosaurs were really quite small;
The young ones, especially, were not very tall.

N is for Noah

N is for **Noah**, his wife, and his kin,
Who, with the animals, also went in.
Dinosaurs outside the ark were all drowned;
That's why as fossils their bones are now found.

O is for Out

O is for **Out** of the ark they all ran,
Once the huge vessel came safely to land.
Stegasaurs, lambeosaurs, nodosaurs, and more;
After the Flood there were dinosaurs galore!

P is for Pronounce

P is for Pronounce: are the names hard for you?
Iguanodon, diplodocus, now how did you do?
Brachiosaurus, tyrannosaurus, and others as well,
What happened to them is the story we'll tell.

Q is for Question

Q is for **Question** – why can't we any more,
Look around and see even one dinosaur?
They're surely all dead, it's as simple as that;
Try to guess why – put on your thinking hat.

R is for Reasons

(wheel labels: HUNTERS, ICE AGE, VOLCANOES, STORMS, DISEASE, DROUGHT, SNOW, ?)

R is for **Reasons** – perhaps there are more;
After the Flood, times were tougher for sure;
Volcanoes and storms, then drought and snow,
Maybe people killed them – they frightened them so.

S is for Section

S is for a **Section** from God's Holy Book;

About a great beast; when he walked the ground shook.

Behemoth, or monster, was this animal's name:

Our word "dinosaur" means almost the same.

T is for Tales

T is for **Tales** that we often hear

About terrible dragons that made men fear.

Maybe these tales could actually be

Stories of dinosaurs men used to see.

U is for Understand

U is for Understand, which we want to do;

The Bible explains the dinosaurs for you.

It also tells how from sin to be saved;

By trusting in Jesus, who rose from the grave.

V is for Very

Adam and Eve

Jonah

David and Goliath

Jesus

If I have told you earthly things, and and ye believe not, how shall ye believe, if I tell you of heavenly things? John 3:12

V is for how **Very** much we can say
We all should read the Bible each day.
Dinosaurs we've proven, are no mystery;
God's Word teaches us true history.

W is for Watchfulness

W is for **Watchfulness**, which we should all learn,
Since some day Jesus, our Lord, will return.
He's going to judge this world once again;
But this time by fire, instead of by rain.

X is for eXcited

X is in **eXcited**, which Christians should be,
One day we know that heaven we'll see.
There'll be no more dying, or crying or pain;
For God our Creator, forever will reign.

Y is for Years

Y is for Years, how long could it be,
Since God made the world for you and for me?
"Probably only six thousand or so,"
Say many good scientists; they ought to know!

Z is for Zeal

Z is for the **Zeal** which people should see,
As we tell the truth about history.
The dinosaurs certainly have not evolved;
Through God's Holy Word, the puzzle is solved!

D is for Dino

A is for Answers from God's Holy Book;
Just open the pages and take a good look.
God created the earth, in space it did hang;
Creation's first day, without a BIG BANG.

B is for Bible, where it says on day 2,
God made the clean air for me and for you.
He divided the waters above and below;
Day 3 comes next, so there we shall go.

C is for Continent, the first dry land,
Which God had made by His Powerful hand.
Then He commanded that all the plants grow;
The third day was truly a beautiful show.

D is for Dinosaur, but you'll have to wait,
'Cause on day four other things God did make.
He formed the sun, the stars, and the moon.
Are you ready? We'll see those dinosaurs soon!

E is for Everything that swims in the seas,
Made on day five, with the birds in the trees.
He also created the great Plesiosaur;
Reading God's Word, we can know this for sure.

F is for Fantastic — that's all we can say,
As we see what God made on this, the sixth day!
Adam and Eve and the pouched kangaroo;
The rest of the animals and dinosaurs, too.

G is for the Garden God specially made,
Where Adam and Eve could always have stayed.
Living in Eden, a world without sin;
What a beautiful place for them to live in.

H is for Hungry, it's how we describe
A big dinosaur with his mouth open wide.
Adam wasn't scared to watch dinosaurs eat,
Because all the creatures ate plants, and not meat.

I is the letter in the middle of s**I**n,
To remind us all of the trouble we're in.
Dinosaurs, people, and the whole universe;
Because of man's sin, God judged with a curse.

J means Just awful — I'm sure we could say
The effects of sin grew worse every day.
Flesh became violent, the Bible reveals.
Were people and creatures now dinosaur meals?

K is for Knowledge, which made Noah sad;
The world would be judged, because people were bad!
God warned he would send a terrible flood
That would cover the world with water and mud.

L is for Listen: Noah knew that he should,
As soon as God said, "Make an ark out of wood.
Take each land animal, two-by-two;
Your family's among the hard-working crew."

M is for Monster like the great dinosaur;
But how could he enter the ark through the door?
Well, many dinosaurs were really quite small;
The young ones, especially, were not very tall.

N is for Noah, his wife, and his kin,
Who, with the animals, also went in.
Dinosaurs outside the ark were all drowned;
That's why as fossils their bones are now found.

O is for Out of the ark they all ran,
Once the huge vessel came safely to land.
Stegasaurs, lambeosaurs, nodosaurs, and more;
After the Flood there were dinosaurs galore!

P is for Pronounce: are the names hard for you?
Iguanodon, diplodocus, now how did you do?
Brachiosaurus, tyrannosaurus, and others as well,
What happened to them is the story we'll tell.

Q is for Question – why can't we any more,
Look around and see even one dinosaur?
They're surely all dead, it's as simple as that;
Try to guess why – put on your thinking hat.

R is for Reasons – perhaps there are more;
After the Flood, times were tougher for sure;
Volcanoes and storms, then drought and snow,
Maybe people killed them – they frightened them so.

S is for a Section from God's Holy Book;
About a great beast; when he walked the ground shook.
Behemoth, or monster, was this animal's name:
Our word "dinosaur" means almost the same.

T is for Tales that we often hear
About terrible dragons that made men fear.
Maybe these tales could actually be
Stories of dinosaurs men used to see

U is for Understand, which we want to do;
The Bible explains the dinosaurs for you.
It also tells how from sin to be saved;
By trusting in Jesus, who rose from the grave.

V is for how Very much we can say
We all should read the Bible each day.
Dinosaurs we've proven, are no mystery;
God's Word teaches us true history.

W is for Watchfulness, which we should all learn,
Since some day Jesus, our Lord, will return.
He's going to judge this world once again;
But this time by fire, instead of by rain.

X is in eXcited, which Christians should be,
One day we know that heaven we'll see.
There'll be no more dying, or crying or pain;
For God our Creator, forever will reign.

Y is for Years, how long could it be,
Since God made the world for you and for me?
"Probably only six thousand or so,"
Say many good scientists; they ought to know!

Z is for the Zeal which people should see,
As we tell the truth about history.
The dinosaurs certainly have not evolved;
Through God's Holy Word, the puzzle is solved!

Be a Part of this Biblical Adventure!

N is for Noah
Trusting God and His Promises
Illustrated by Jeff Albrecht
Ken & Mally Ham
978-0-89051-702-4

Learning to Trust in God & His Promises

Think of these unique books as "step one" in crafting a child's biblical worldview! In a fun and informative way, these three titles share biblical insights with wondrous artwork that is fun for kids and appreciated by parents and teachers alike. Using rhyme to present essential truth, these books provide structured learning encouraged with important words, biblical concepts, and verses. The colorful illustrations combined with the text share God's Word in ways a child can truly understand!

Also Available

A is for Adam
the Gospel from Genesis
Ken & Mally Ham
978-0-89051-625-6

D is for Dinosaur
Noah's Ark and the Genesis Flood
Illustrated by Jeff Albrecht
Ken & Mally Ham
978-0-89051-642-3

Ken Ham
President/CEO and Founder of Answers in Genesis, The Creation Museum, and the Ark Encounter

Master Books®
A Division of New Leaf Publishing Group
www.masterbooks.com

THINK BIGGER

ARK ENCOUNTER

ArkEncounter.com

Williamstown, KY
(south of Cincinnati)